Ricky Roogle

The
Super
MAZE BOOK
for Am@ng.us Fans

Bibliografische Information der Deutschen Nationalbibliothek:
Die Deutsche Nationalbibliothek verzeichnet diese Publikation in der Deutschen
Nationalbibliografie; detaillierte bibliografische
Daten sind im Internet über http://dnb.dnb.de abrufbar.

Herstellung und Verlag: BoD – Books on Demand, Norderstedt
ISBN: 9783752657753

Help Astronaut to get to the exit.

Exit

Solution of Maze 1

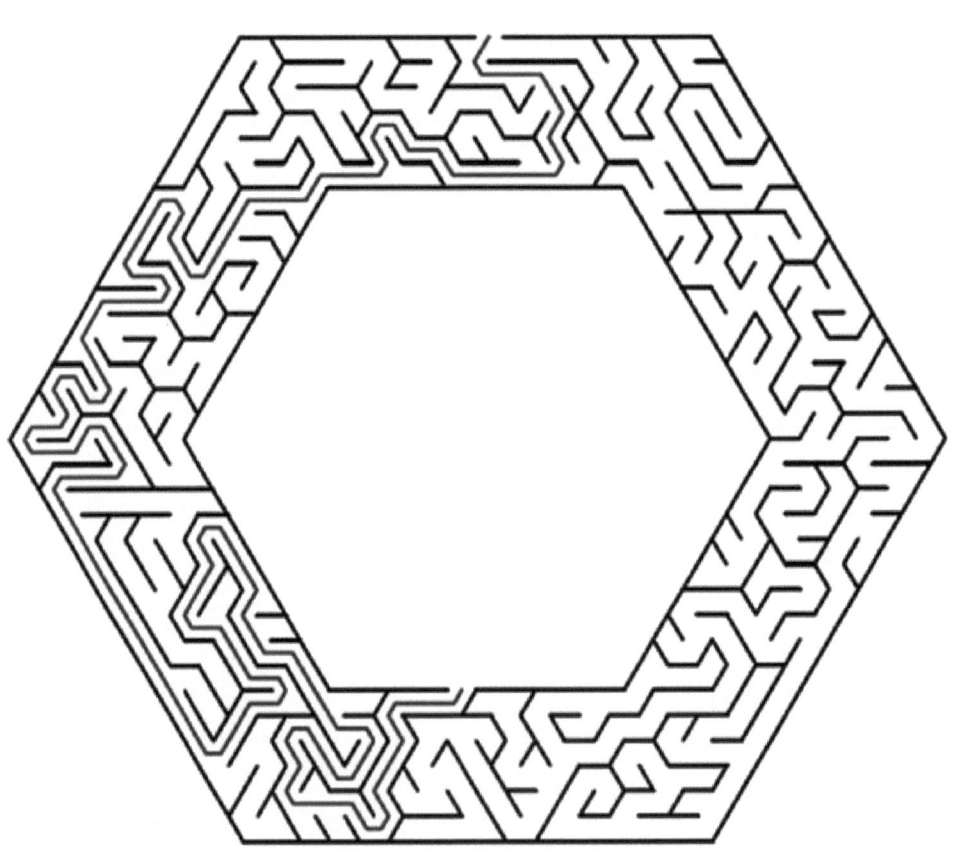

Help Banana
to find his
hamster.

Solution of Maze 2

Help Police Officer
to find Ellie.

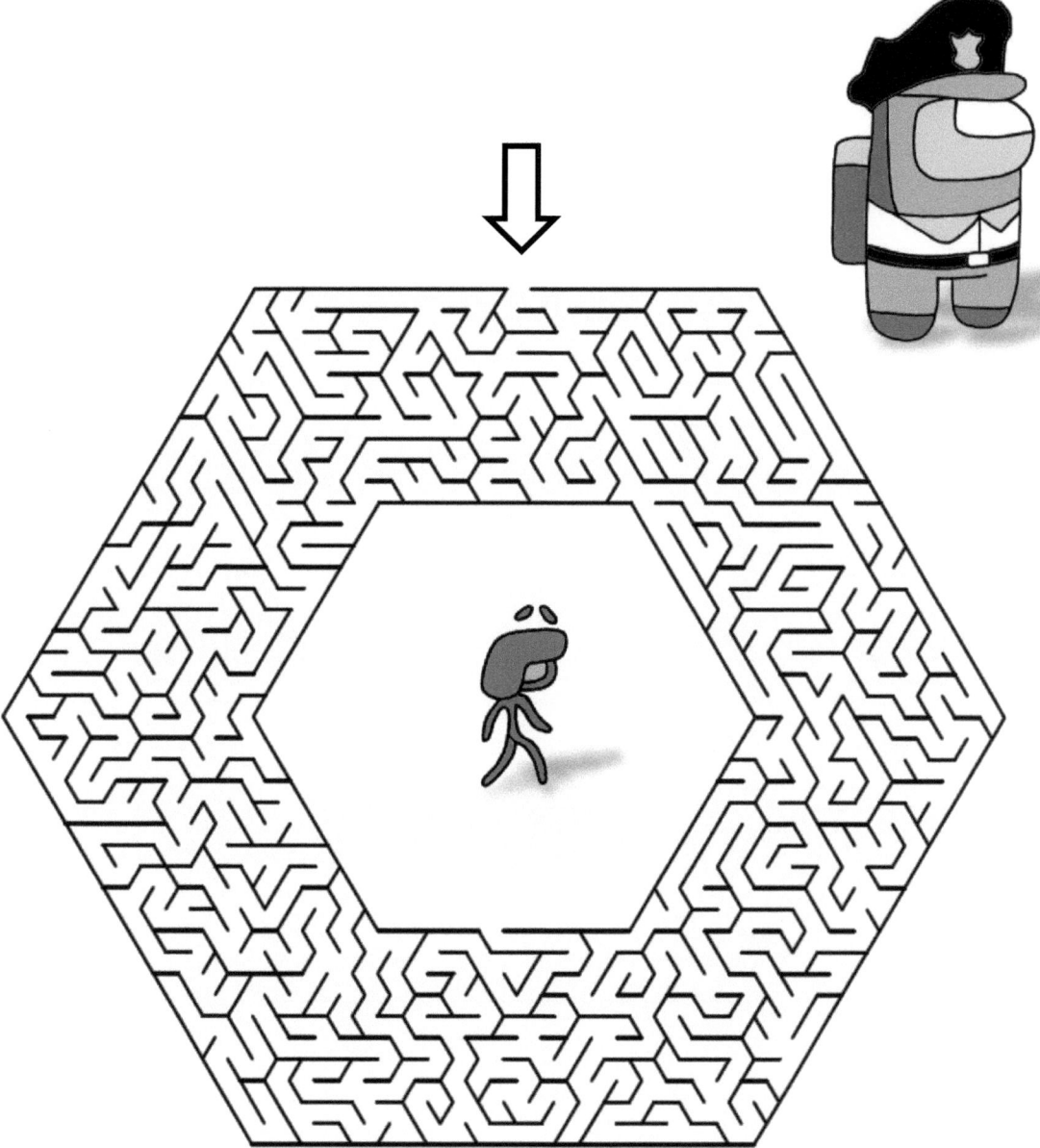

Solution of Maze 3

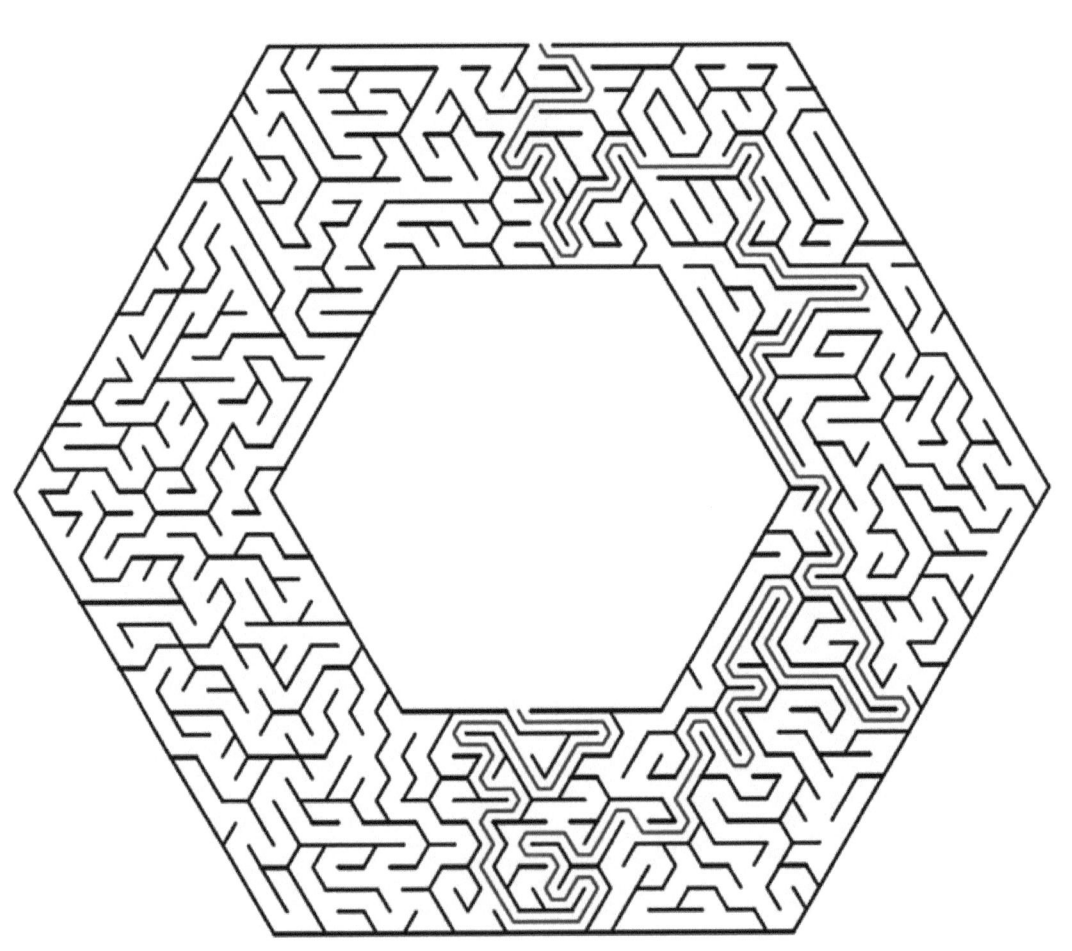

Help the Crewmate to find Brainslug.

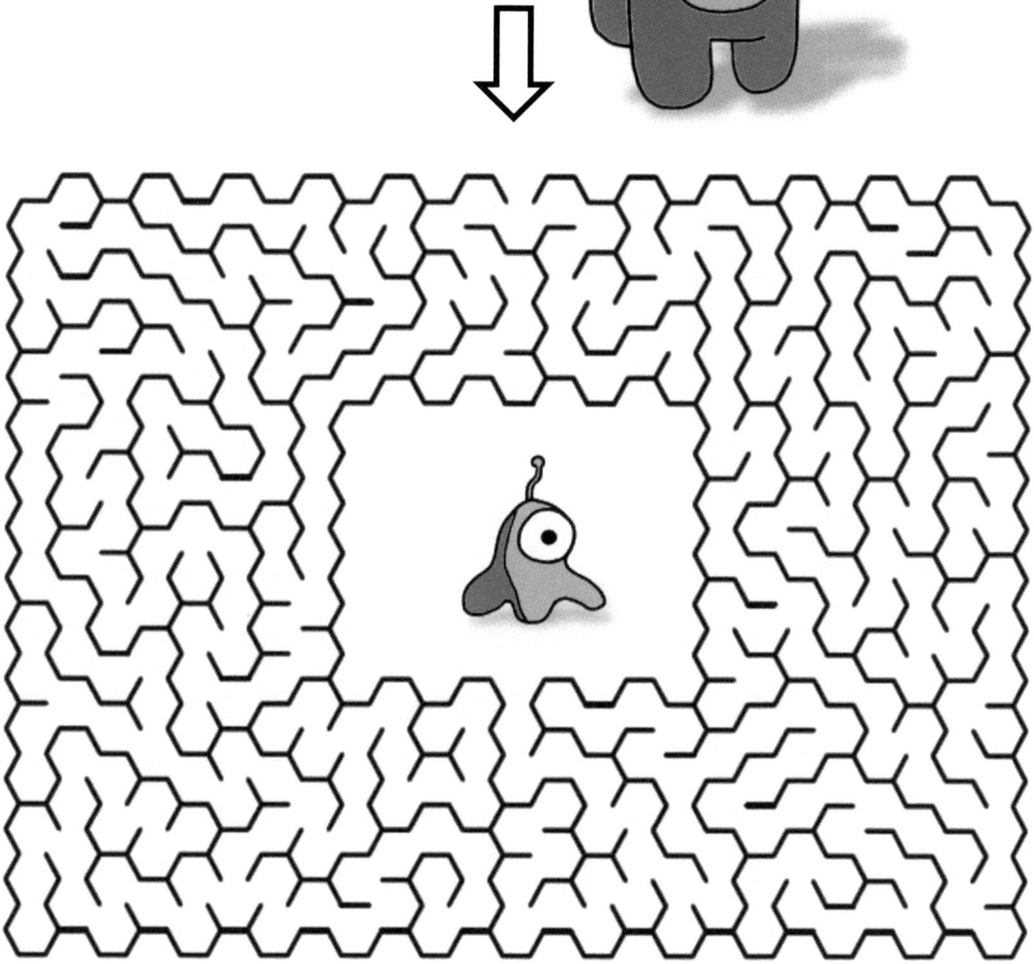

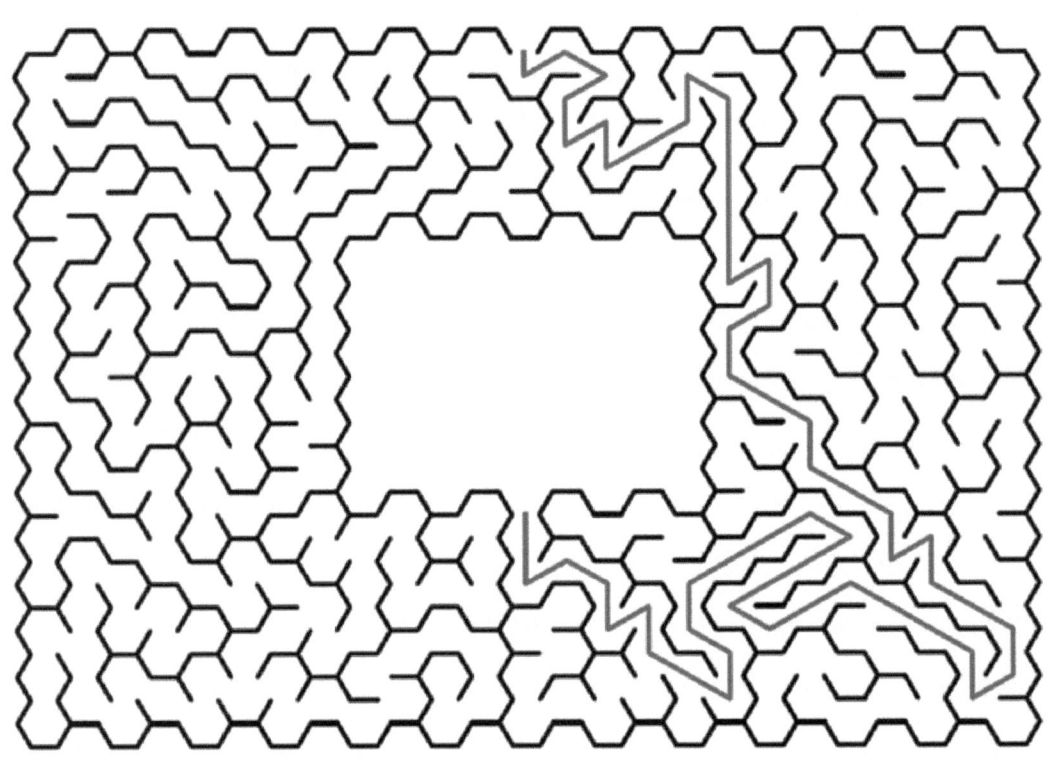

Help the Impostor to get to his ufo.

5

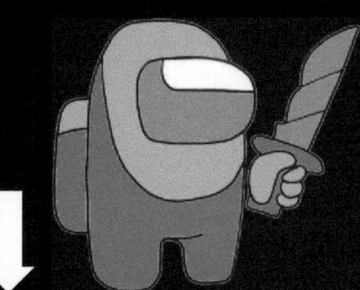

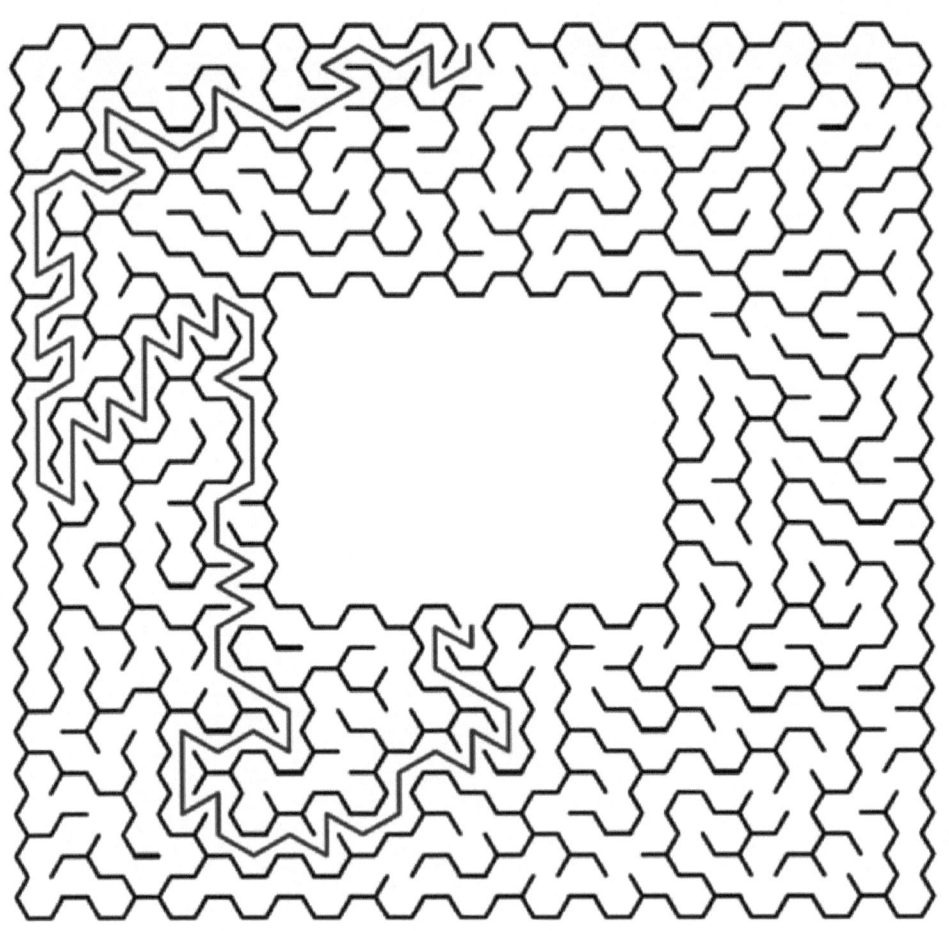

Help Flower to find her dog.

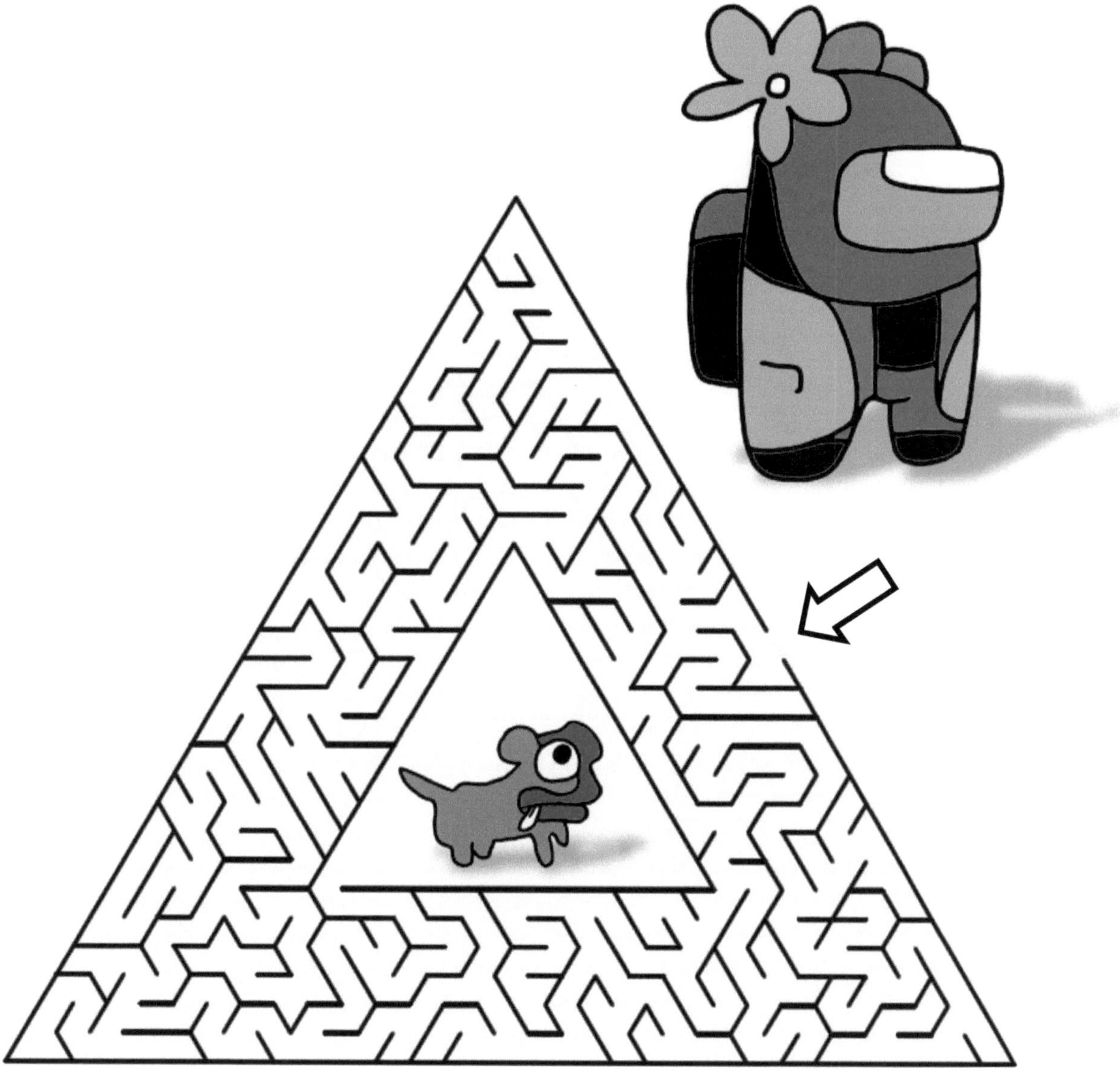

Solution of Maze 6

7

Help the crewmate
to get to his hamster.

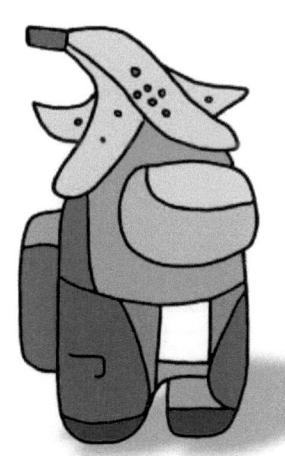

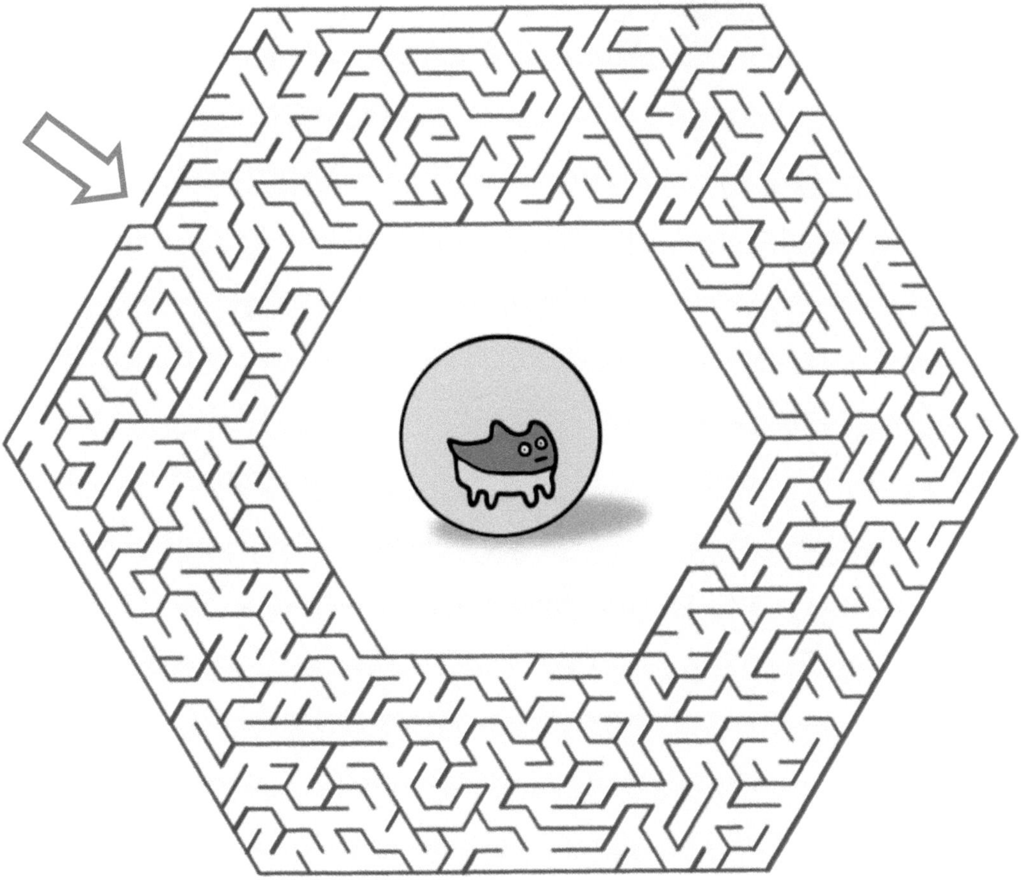

Solution of Maze 7

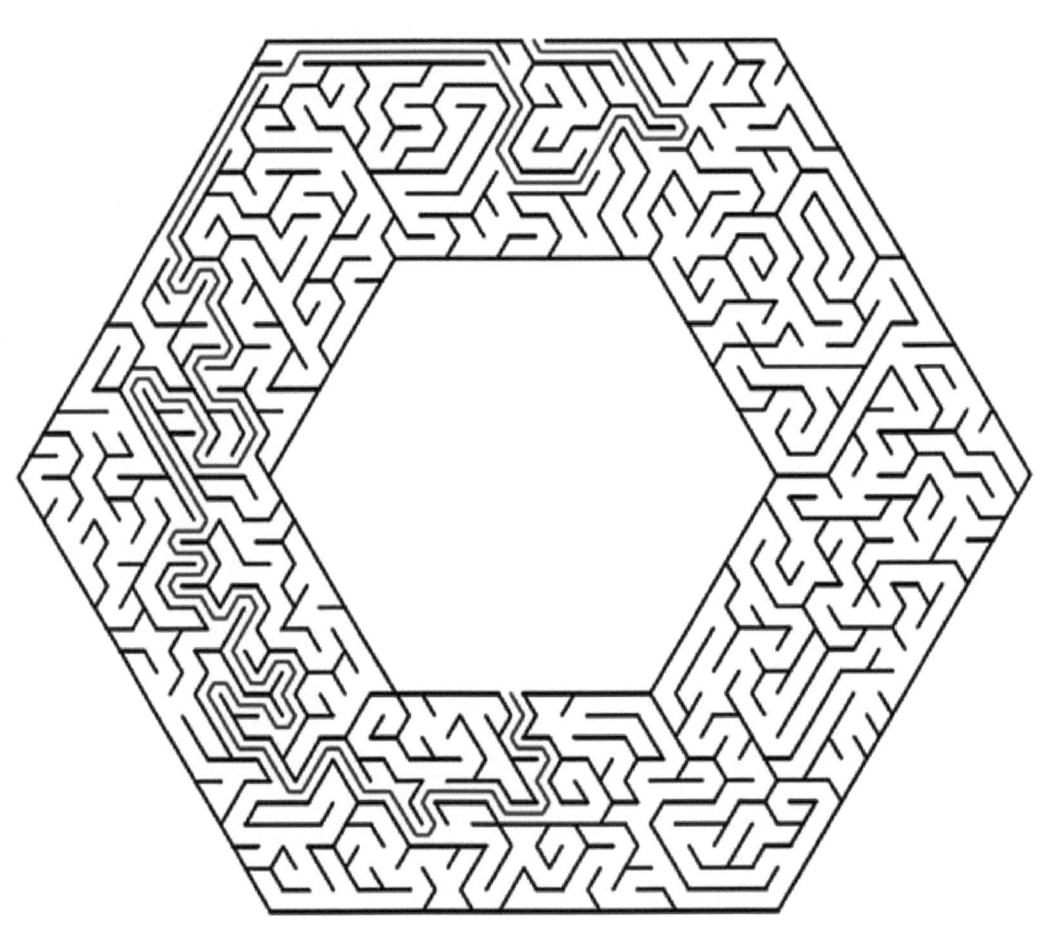

Help Father
Christmas to
find Bedcrab.

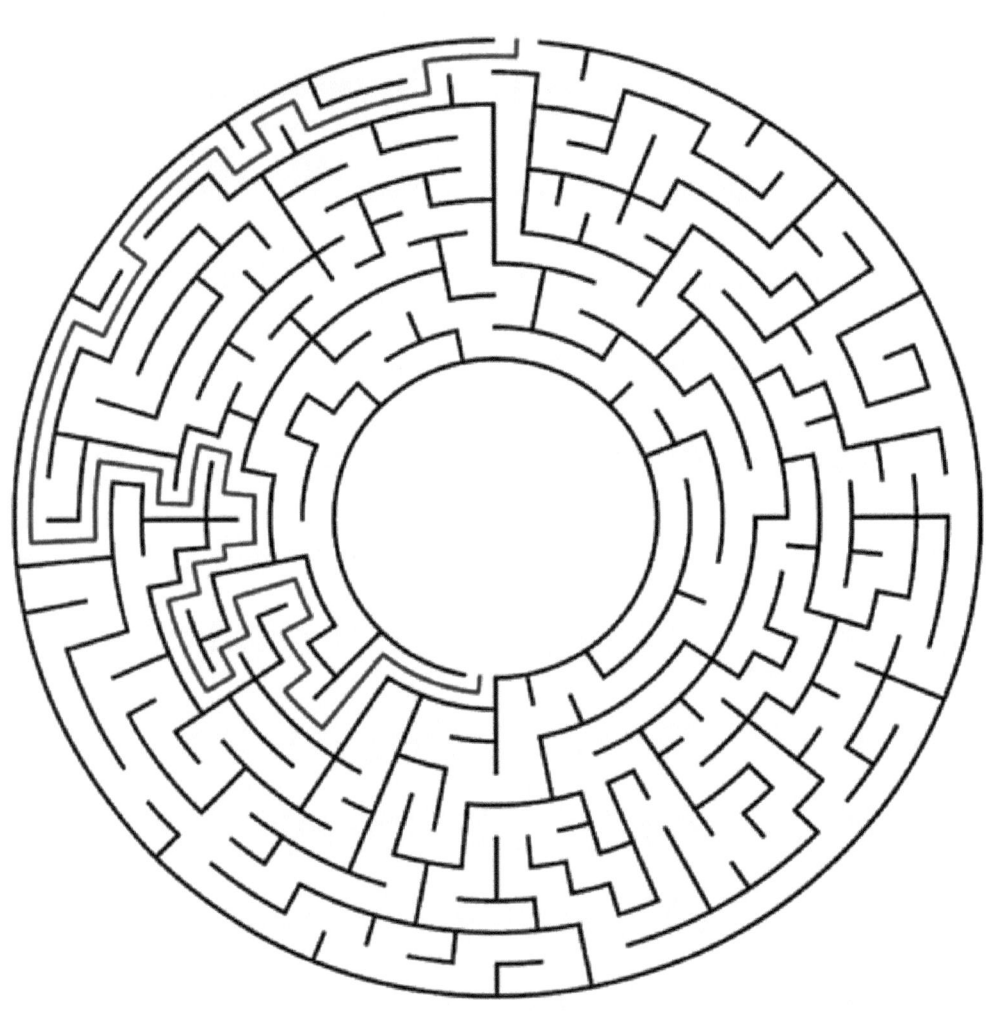

9

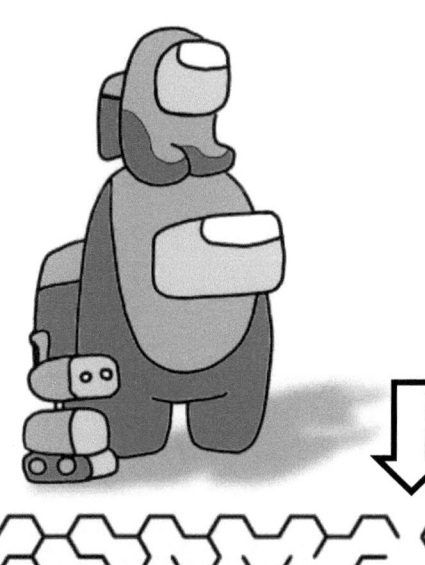

Help the crewmate to get to the second robot.

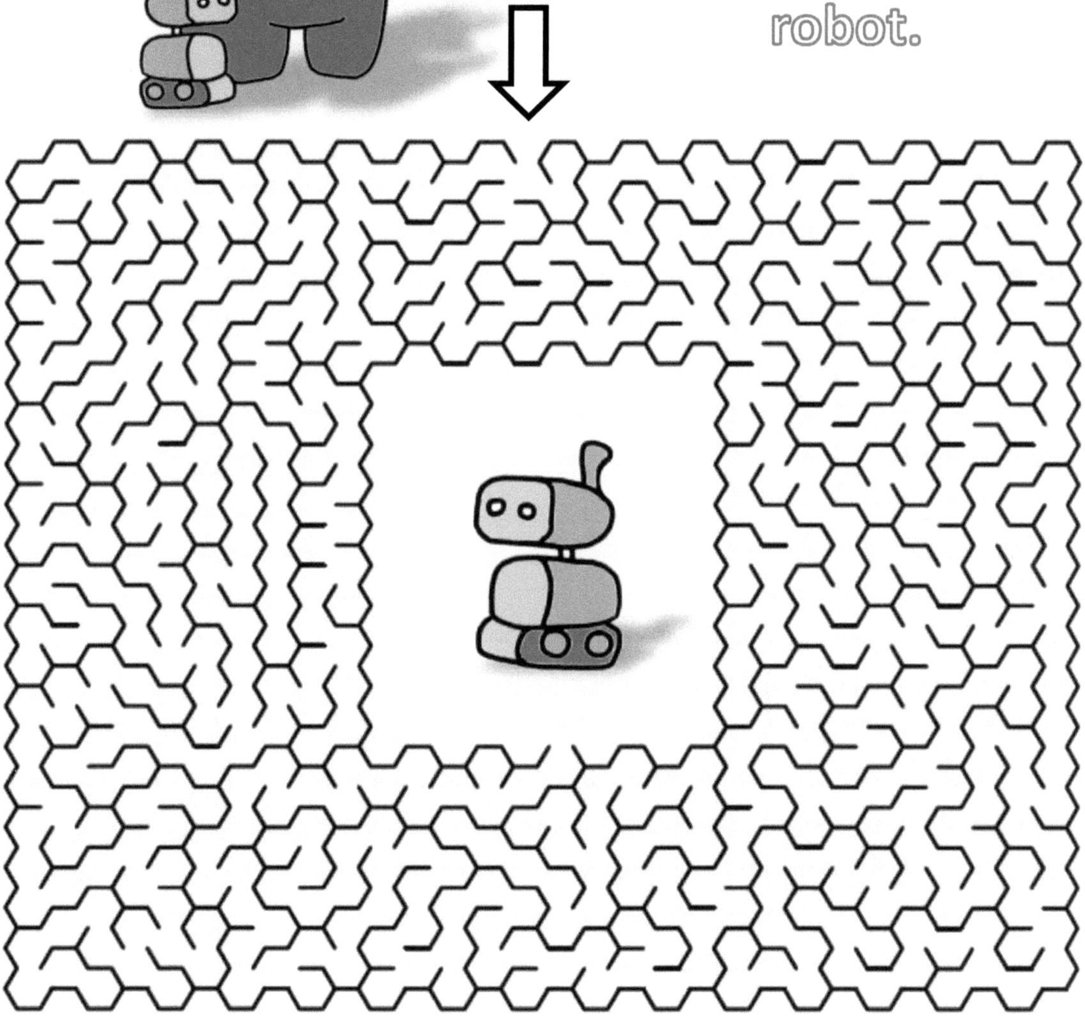

Solution of Maze 9

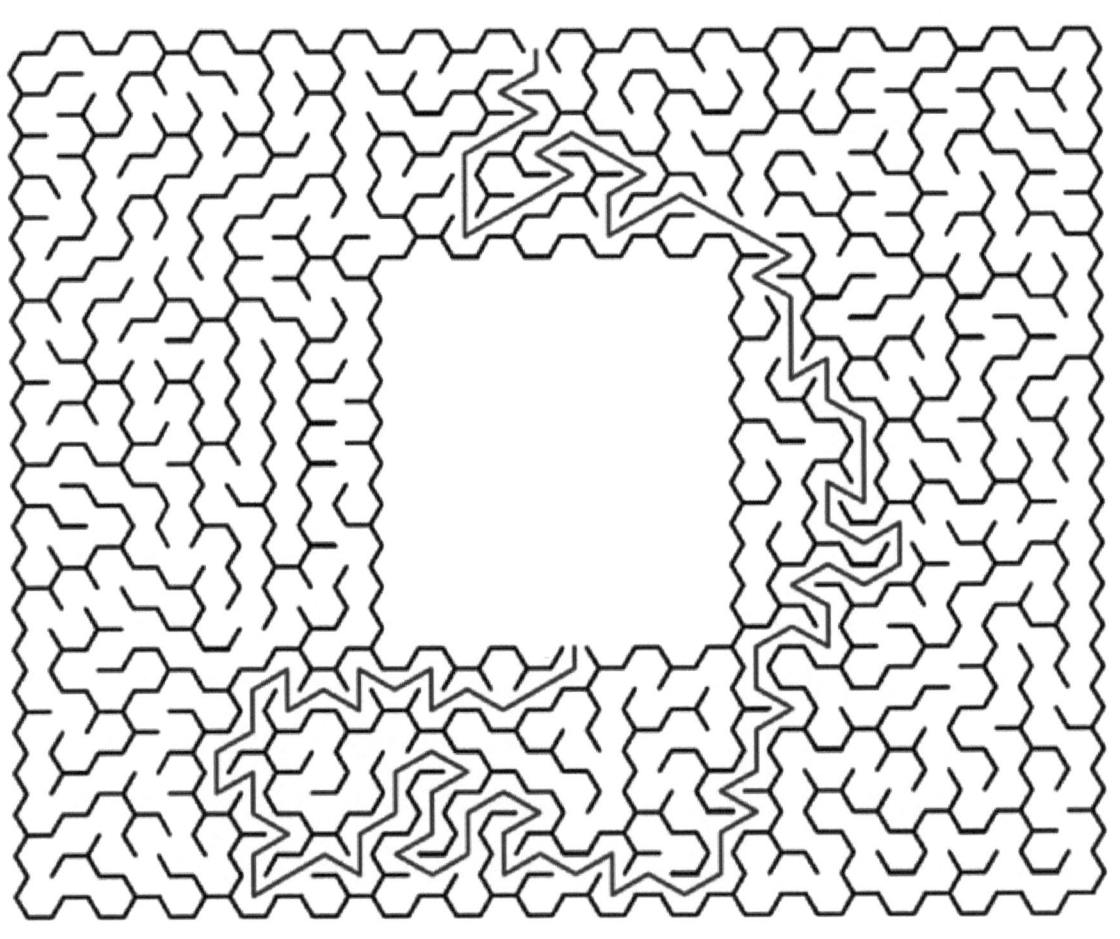

Help Pilot
to call a
report.

Help the crewmate
to get to his
second Squig.

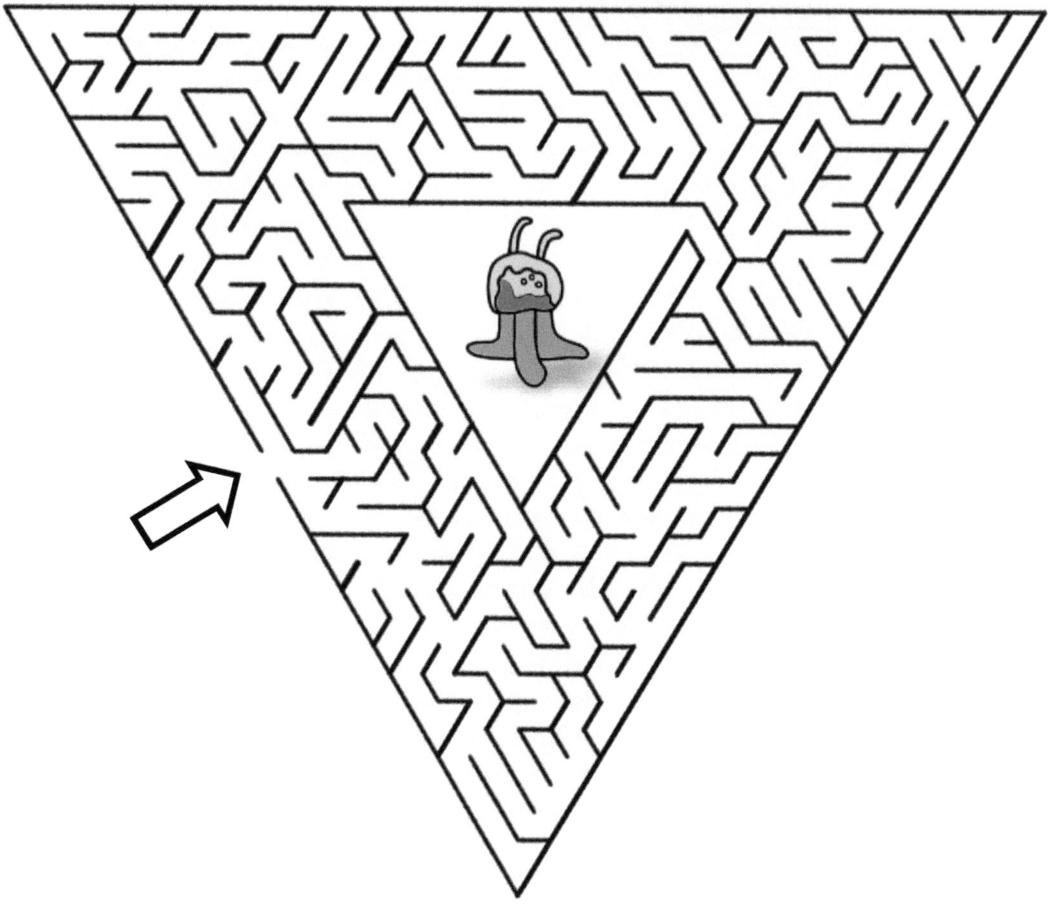

Solution of Maze 11

Help Mister Egg to find Ellie.

Solution of Maze 12

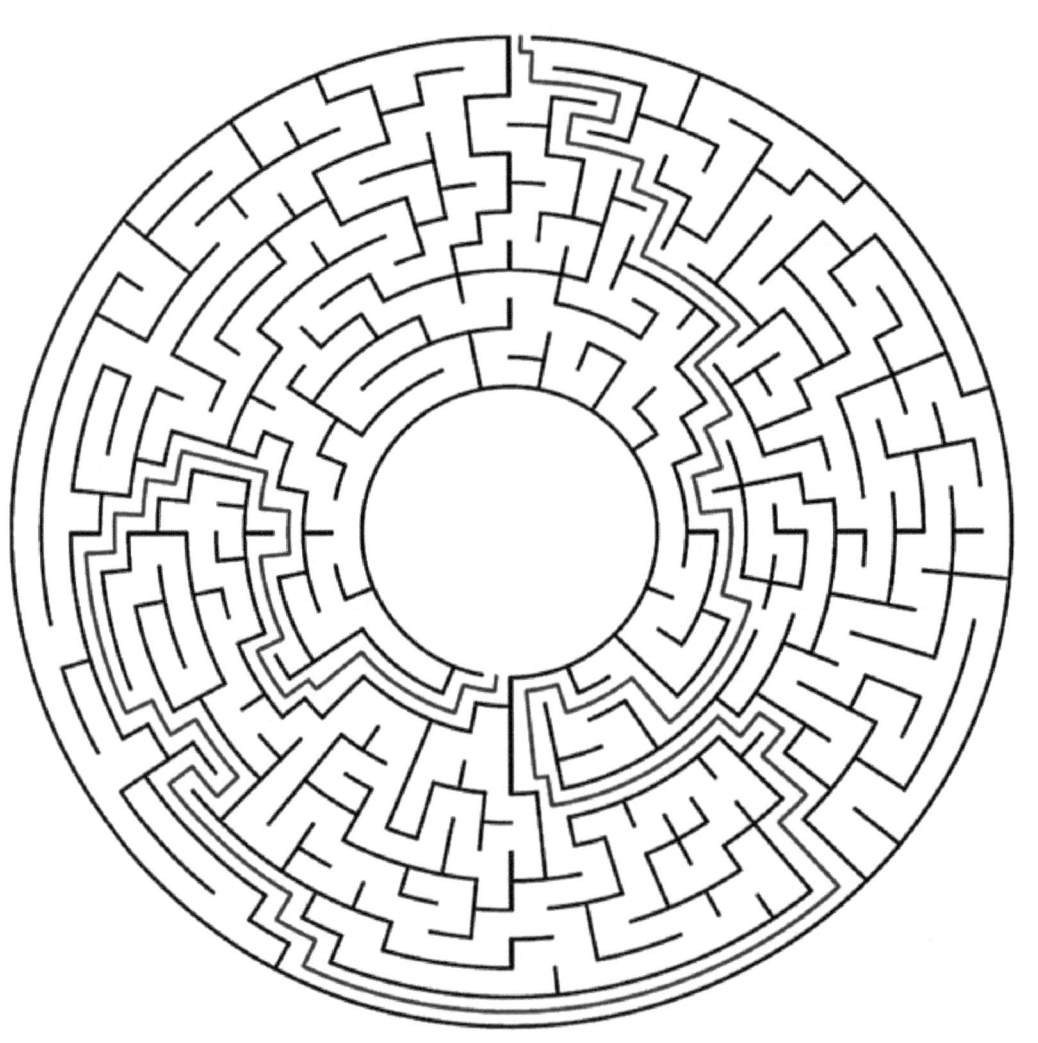

Help the crewmate to get to the exit.

Exit

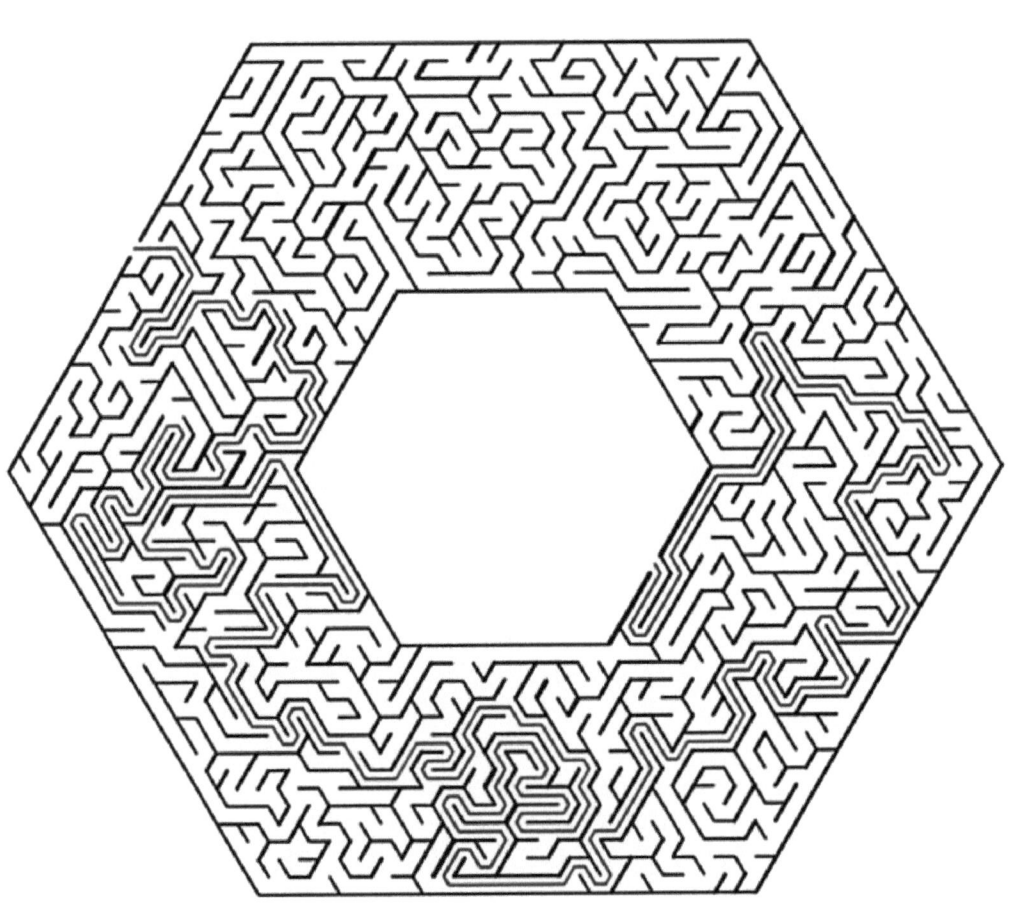

Help Henry to find its crewmate.

Help Hockeymask
to get to the place
of sabotage.

Solution of Maze 15

Help crewmate to find the brother of the hamster.

Solution of Maze 16

Help the doctor to get to the exit.

Exit

Solution of Maze 17

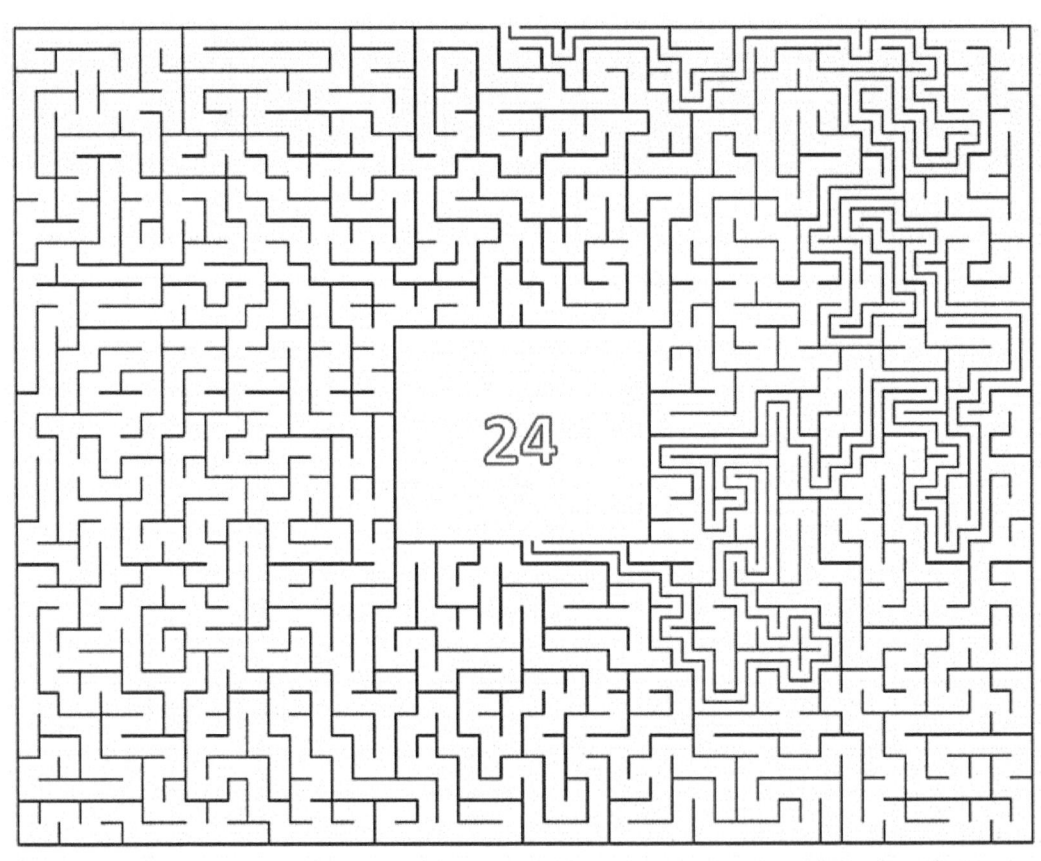

18

Help crewmate to find the second Brainslug.

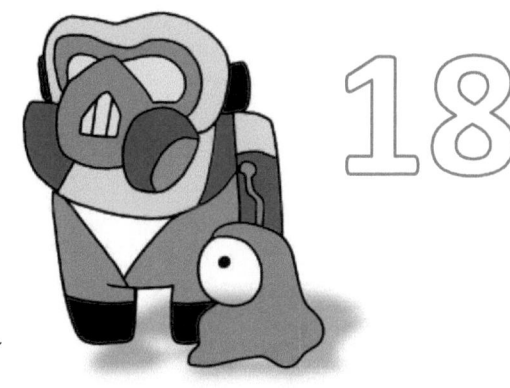

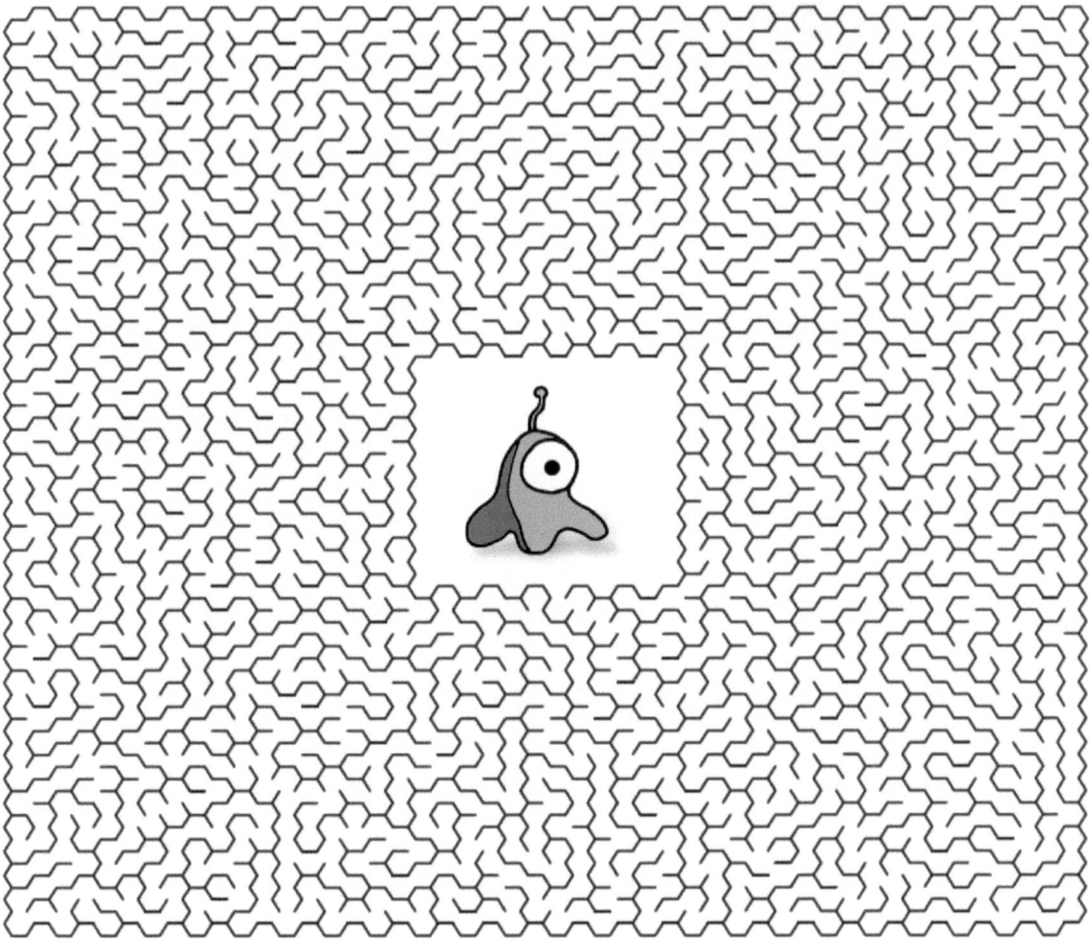

Solution of Maze 18

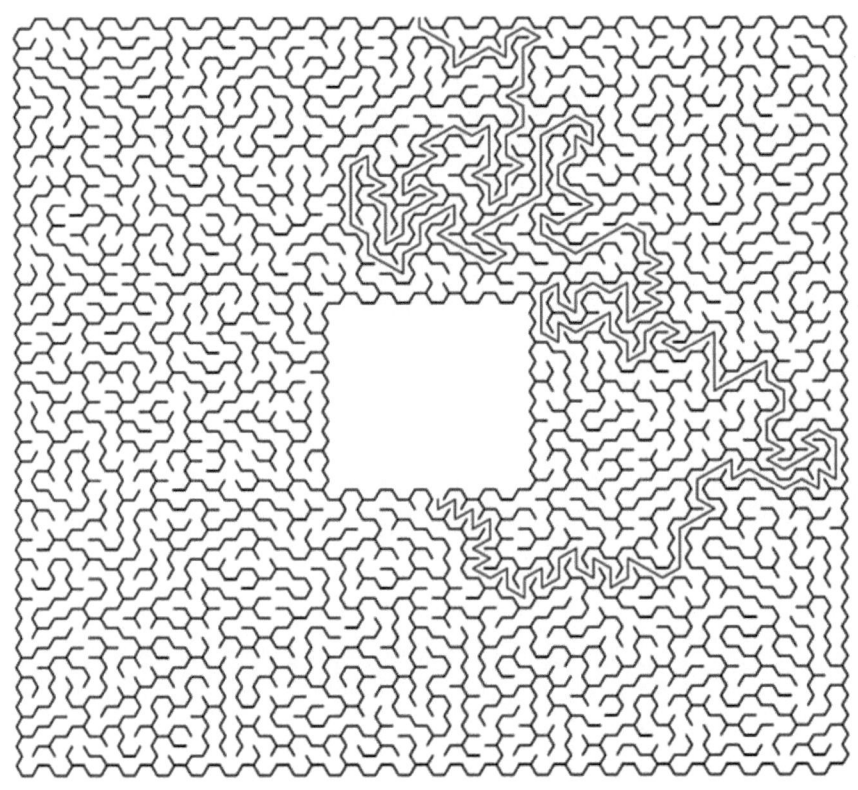